War Of Words

Verses Of The Broken, Volume 20

Adam Levon Brown

Published by Adam Levon Brown Poetry, 2024.

War of Words

Adam Levon Brown

War of Words
She V2
Mind Scrape
Queer Confessional
The Pursuit of Joy
Broken English
Pale Side of Noon
1010101 Declaration
Nuclear Prisoners
Trumped
Atlas Shrugs Because he's Cold
The Artist
Third-World Panic
Whispers of Death
Foresight
Untitled
Melodious Misanthropy
Death of M
Light Dancer
The Movement of the Homo Sapiens
Myth of Freedom
Gifts of Burden
Grandfather Neptune
Thy Kingdom Come
Seeking Solace
Night on the Streets
Neoliberal Narcotics
Life Twisted
Misery Hates Company
The Numbness Pervades
The Solitude of Bukowski
Mirage

Comrades in Crime
RepubliKANT
Imagination amalgamation
For Sale
Soulful Sondering
Manic in the Afternoon
Fences
Optical Illusion
Self-Portrait
Serpentine Regret
The Heart Must be Opened

War of Words

Bullets fired
From your mouth
Penetrate poisoned
hearts in a waking dream

Incendiary rounds spouted
with sniper precision
aimed at the jugular.

It's time to wrestle
the industrialized steel
That you've fashioned
from your vile rhetoric.

Shotgun blasts pierce
The stained flesh and
will forever meld with
bone, creating

Androids for the next
Holy war

Dodging your arsenal
of verbiage,

I take refuge in my
own words while building
my vocabulary

She V2

She was the cosmos fit
With a Molotov face and
A bullet-stained body

She had a way with words
That would leave you feeling
Stretched like a summer day

She could kiss like a hand grenade,
Exploding with fervor; the kind
Of kiss you dream about 10 years later

She laughed like a thunderstorm
That would last for days

She left me for a golden
ticket to the fast-growing
high-rise in the blooming sky.

Mind Scrape

My mind is a knife aimed at the throat of hypocrisy
My mind is an arrow protruding from the chest of patriarchy
My mind is a net within which the death throes of capitalism can be heard
My mind is the Plebes setting fire to Rome
My mind's retractable steps in the journey to find where we went wrong
My mind is revolution in the hands of all who listen

Queer Confessional

Thinking about men
has only seemed natural
to me for 21 days and 6 hours.

Years spent denying my very core
and reveling in the fact
that I could do it.

The war has ended
and the dust has settled.

Cobwebs in my heart
have been replaced
with a renewed vigor.

I don't know where to go
from here, but my eyes
are set to the sky.

I am free.

The Pursuit of Joy

The crimson stains
of a blood once filled
with power

Has regurgitated onto
the floor of regret

The platelets drip
into the sewer of
identity crises

The platelets drip
into the mouth
of syphilitic vampires

Mountains are moved
daily while Sisyphus
struggles with one rock

At the bottom of the hill
is where all life begins
and ends

Broken English

Stormy clouds
pervade

Consonants of differing
magma

Which stem from
multiple

Scenarios in a fluent
language

That is only understood by
cosmonauts

Pale Side of Noon

Dark Wintry haven
for trench coats in black

Mirrored sunglasses kiss the
falling snowflakes

Icicles form on the brows
of ghastly visages;

Eyebrows seeking
redemption in the pull

of the moon.
Distance covered by

Drugged feet in
the snow.

Danse Macabre
of Winter's teeth

The Sun melts away
the beginning and the end.

1010101 Declaration

<A=href>
Slipping
Slipped

Sipping the
marrow
from the bones
Results in paralysis

Honeyed/ lies
lead/ to/ the
bitterest/ heartache
<imgsource=Https://moltenlavawithwords

Italic porcelain
Bold Words for a poet
<end>

Nuclear Prisoners

T r i p p I n g
on syllables
Pontificated Piousness
POISONS

~~Coriander and hemlock for the prisoner!~
Precious moments make for Hollywood cash

Drift
Drifting
.....Drifted

Acidosis of the mind splits atoms
BOOM!

Trumped

Stockholm syndrome
has never been more apparent

Reality television locked and shut
within a cellophane bubble

Cultural wasteland of
discarded dreams and ideas

The hopes that people
once shared have been
brought to the guillotine
and executed

A live show for all to see.
Now is moment to prepare
for the time when they
begin watching you

Atlas Shrugs Because he's Cold

The flames of a nation
dwindle down to a single
candle flame

Engulfed by ferocious winds
in the anamorphic chaos
of the times

What will happen to
the disabled?

Penniless and forgotten
left to rot behind political
bars of ineptitude
What will happen to
Muslims?

Shipped off, physically
branded by the hot iron
of injustice

What will happen
to this country?

What will happen
to this country?
What will happen
to this country?

The Artist

The canvas bends
to the enigmatic force
of her brush stroke
Hues blend and swirl
in obsidian fashion

Splatters and visions
pour forth in
erratic movements

She paints a moonless
sky for all of the
darkness in her life

Trees crooked and barbed
for the betrayal she
has experienced

Water polluted and grimy
for the many painful tears
she has shed

She finishes with her signature
in the bottom
right hand corner

And proceeds to
light the

painting on fire

Cleansing the
impurities
and starting anew

Third-World Panic

Hope bows to the misery
which seeps from the pores
Of miscalculations.

In broken dreams,
The sun rises and sets.

The distance between kaleidoscope
eyes and trust in false neon idols
never seems to end.

Cotton and ink;
Drips with the blood
of a fellowship which
Will never see

The twilight of peace

Whispers of Death

The candle is lit;
And the serendipitous
Moment shone high
Through the mountains

Call it fate
Call it destiny
Call it a journey to
The side of life that few
Have cared to notice

Call it whatever you want,
But never doubt its power over you

All who have felt its chilled embrace
Have seen the visage of a torn down idol
Catching- Holding-

Praying- Hoping-
Living- Dying-
Dying-
Dying-
Dying-
Dying.

Foresight

Deserted island
of macular degeneration
Residing in Irises.

Bloomed declarations
of agape love.

Dilated magnificence
Pulls gravity to a dead halt.

Seeing through supernova
euphoria, branches of light
reflect the state of consciousness.

Untitled

Devilish serpent
of Nefarious
design

Spit your venom
into the eyes of
the saints

Mercurial messiah
of misshapen
maladies

Rest your halo
on gold-tipped
wings

Mold the iron until
its strong enough to
break my will

When the curfew
ends, there will
be a story to tell.

Melodious Misanthropy

Rabid ruby eyes
Drink the darkness
with a mouth full of
broken glass

Storm-blackened
window panes
screech their ivory
cries of death

Monsters hide
from themselves
in frothy
alcohol

A sip of Hemlock
drowned in
Vivacious fervor

Strike the mallet upon
the oak as this
judgment
has passed.

Death of M

I saw you struck
down within a dream.

I fell to my knees
and cried,

I fell down and
died;

One thousand deaths
of the setting Sun.

Light Dancer

The meandering of
Cosmic vibrations
enrapture the amber moon
in Mahogany fashion.

The dance of the
Cerulean waves storming
The beige sand dunes whisper sinfully.

A kiss of light upon the
Honeysuckle gives birth to
Fragrant mistakes of a time long gone.

Time settles in for an ancient sleep
And closes the rust-laden doors
within my tattered mind.

The Movement of the Homo Sapiens

The flow of the masses
waxes and wanes
with the passing of
the clock

Clock in.

Toiling in
the sinew of
society

Clock out.

Grab some cheap
dinner and prepare
for the next day

Cars appear as
bees going and returning
from destination to destination
to destination

Myth of Freedom

Individual
self conforms
to the whim of
society

Passions, hobbies, playing
all seem to take a
back seat

To the performance
one must play
in order to fit in
and survive

There are rules,
there are dictums,
there are enforced guidelines

No person in society is free,
as they are made to play a part
in someone else's show

Gifts of Burden

I carry around my misery
like a bag of presents

I present them to everyone
I meet along the arduous journey

Suffering for you, self-pity for them
and a bit of darkness to top it all off

By giving these gifts away, I am
freed to experience positive emotions

By giving these gifts away, I can
relate to you in ways that simple

Consumerism fails to do so.
I will walk the lonely road
and settle in silence when
the day is over and done.

Grandfather Neptune

Milky Way Galactic Showers
juxtaposed
against my falling tears-

When will the last star fall?

The planets of this galaxy are stuck in orbit,
wishing that they could take the Sun's place.

The Sun stands firmly upon
its throne,

Stomping out hope for
any other to reign supreme.

Biding its time and making its rounds,
Saturn has wrestled to break free,
but has only been met with abject failure.

Neptune in its Sapphire wisdom looks on
and wonders why the rest have not accepted
their fate.

Thy Kingdom Come

Black Lotus eyes foresee
gold-tinted Abalone shells
Cased within
velvet-lined caskets.

Ebony correlations
slink to and fro
On a bronze ship
headed for the hazy horizon.

Some call it Valhalla while
others ignore it altogether.

I prefer to set my sails
of Byzantine glory and
bask in the timelessness
that this life has to offer.

Seeking Solace

Obsidian meadows
permeate
the sunken
psyche

As foragers of
silk seek solace
in the virtue of their
false idols

Scavengers prowl
the marrowless
bones
of our planet

In search of pontificated
piousness within the realm
of jeweled nights and
solar-scorched days

What they don't know,
is that what they seek
resides inside their own
blood-shaven bodies

Night on the Streets

Stripping the molded
paint off of street art
results in

Anaphylactic
earthquakes of Divine
magnitude

Halcyon hallucinations
highlight the harrowing
adventure

Smash the bottles
of beer on the wall
and rejoice in the madness

Neoliberal Narcotics

Dogma
forced down
the throats of
the disenfranchised.

Cultural genocide plagued
with colonialist ways
of thinking

From food to language,
entire groups of people
Are wiped from the
face of the globe

They become a token
talking point in History
classes

But at least they
follow our ways
Because they're ultimately
superior, right?
Dogma
forced down
the throats of
the disenfranchised

Life Twisted

Life twisted-

Symbiosis

Death Ignored-

Mutation
Ripping the

threads
and pulling apart
Dreams in which

the dreamer knows
the outcome

*

Breaking needles

stabbed into the eyes
of morality
Stained and tattered

pages ripped from
the phone book
Numbers divided

that resemble past
fortuitous events

Misery Hates Company

It's not that I
don't love you.

You must understand
that I've made loneliness
A lifestyle

I am so broken
that tears no longer come.

You must understand
that the Sun is just a
contorted memory.

Darkness is my truth
And I plan on telling it.

Fly away, my dove of light.

The Numbness Pervades

Dead eyes can
only see so far

When the vultures
come to feast

There will be carrion
that will resist

They will resist
but die trying

Such is the darkness
that swallows my psyche

An enigma of a black
hole trapping my spirit
In its chains of misery.

Life succumbs to lies
and bones of the celestial
become numb

Death is your shadow

that follows

And In the end, there
is only numb

The Solitude of Bukowski

Living in drunken
squalor

Rats infest the broken-doored
broom closets

Taking drags from a leper-made
cig while bitching about the horse
races of long past

Burrowing his eyebrows deep
into a scowl

As he looks through mahogany
venetian blinds at the outside world
Solitude was always his friend.

Don't mess with the rest
and you will die like the best

Mirage

Politics
Politricks
Polatricks
Parlourtricks
Parlour Tricks

Comrades in Crime

Another steroid abusing chauvinist
plastered next to an anorexic
Barbie doll. They look like a
cardboard cutout at a planet
Hollywood museum.

Next in line,
bonehead and twig girl numbers 5,026 and 5,027.

The cliche is so deeply
embedded that it sucks the
very oxygen from the brains
that absorb it.

The naive masses
watch the same shit over and
over and over again; they
want to be like these caricatures
of human beings, and they
will do anything to
achieve that goal.

Pills for this,
shakes for that.

The snake oil salesmen
capitalize on naivety.

The soul sucking "entertainment
the industry pays for their ads.

The cycle of turning a person
with dreams into yet another statistic continues

RepubliKANT

I'm no political Jesus
I won't die for your sins
When you refuse to give visas.
While poor people die in the street
and the poorest shuffle their feet
To the death ring of war
Killing those they abhor;
Because of nationalist brainwashing
Poor, young people die for lies
while the old and rich keep on a cashing
In on the density of the masses,
who are lost in the face of greed.
Another war, another day passes
while most are left fighting for need.
I will not sponsor said terrorism
This republic is caught in a schism.

Imagination amalgamation

Imagine
if people gathered to fight injustice
like people line up for the new Iphone.

Imagine
If people spent that money
on building up their communities.

Imagine
If people stormed stores
to provide food for the Homeless
and hungry on Black Friday.

Imagine
A world where borders
were nothing but invisible
lines, blinding us from
seeing our kin.

Imagine
A world where prisoners
were given help.

Imagine

A world where
the term mental illness
was widely understood.

For Sale

Poet for sale
As cheap as you can
get them

Poet for sale
As the masses
march their march
of endless suffering

Poet for sale
They march back
to their little hole
that they call a home
and keep up with
the Kardashians

Poet for sale
The echoes go unheard
as the poet is just one
more thing for sale;

One more voice
among the sea of
endless chatter

Chalk it up as another
story of Capitalism
and it's inevitable
erosive nature

Society is its victim
as it slowly sucks
the last free thought
into its greedy, ill-shaped
mouth

Soulful Sondering

To lift a spirit
is to challenge
the very threads
of fate.

You are telling
the universe
that you do not
agree with current
conditions.

You are sending
positive vibes
through someone
and calling the cosmos
out on its error.

To lift a spirit
is a protest
against everything
working against
that being.

Let us lift each other

with our words
and actions.

Manic in the Afternoon

Mountains jutting from
ground space

Pull at the axis
of my disenfranchised
body

Rushes of euphoria
envelop me in arms
of words unspoken

Synapse broken;
brain on overdrive

I guess that's what I get
for thinking that I could
outrun the darkened visage
that is life

Fences

Caged within
are the hopes
and dreams of
flesh and blood

Yearning to
be at peace
in a world
that doesn't
want to acknowledge
their existence

Sweat and tears
bursting through
the cortex that
is life

Self-sufficiency
burdened
at the top of the
hill

Where vision
is lost on gold

and compassion
is lost to greed
rip open the
fences that
keep so many
from shelter
and solace

Let their voices
and dreams be
heard

Optical Illusion

Tainted respite
Of terrified eyes

Wiping away
The granules
Of morbid Fascination

Preemptive
Strike on
Nerve to pale bone
Misshapen Mortuaries

Lie mold-ridden
In the macular
Degeneration
Of molecular Misfiring

Semblance
Of light
Permeates
The reaches Of
the abyss

That is the

Cornucopia
Of sight

Self-Portrait

If I were to paint myself
the hues would speak of pain

Doused in red and black,
crimson ire soaking

the bed sheets of the mind
with sorrowful cries

Blended with narcissistic
cacophony in ears too shadow-filled to hear

Lies and guilt overshadow
the face, with lines too deep to care

The canvas is tarred and mold-ridden
from nicotine stains and a tired heart

The hands burnt red from
catching colds stripped of pride

The eyes a pitiful stare
off into the abyss which never stares back

The mouth, a lost child prying
lips open, hoping to speak

The hair, tangled with four
regretted seasons, locked to the sky

Serpentine Regret

Sun-dried regrets
slither around my
naked eyes

Poison personified,
as supple as teardrop pain

Egg shells walk on
all fours, cracking
like spilled moonlight

Chaotic stars
born from remnants
of skin shed

Fangs dripping
into meadowlark skies

The bite will never cease,
only punishing deeper,
the words left untouched

The Heart Must be Opened

Sun whispers
explode my ears
Into shattered remains
which drift into cacophonous
resplendence in the eve of time

Butterscotch memories
wake me up to new beginnings

Yearning for a world untouched
by the phantom fingers
of greed and malice

Longing for unity
within the self
while fighting beasts
with teeth still bared
waiting to strike heartseeds
yet to be planted

Trust begins to feel
like a misnomer caught
inside of a dangling modifier
Fear ensues, bringing
waves of ear snapping anxiety

Until Love once
again firmly

plants itself
into the dusk
of remembrance

Don't miss out!

Visit the website below and you can sign up to receive emails whenever Adam Levon Brown publishes a new book. There's no charge and no obligation.

https://books2read.com/r/B-A-FTOQ-ABKEE

Did you love *War Of Words*? Then you should read *(Un)Broken*[1] by Adam Levon Brown!

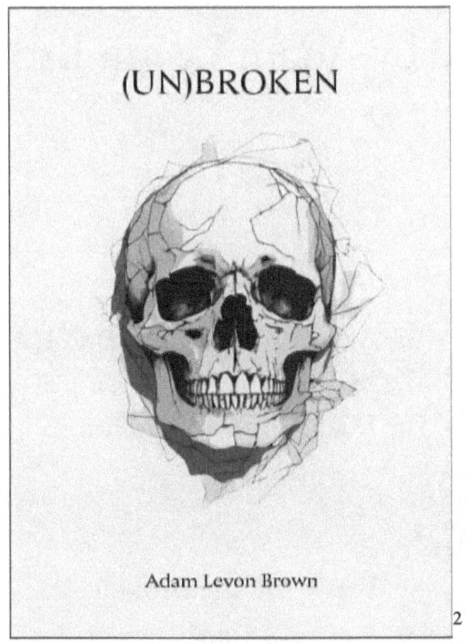

[2]

(Un)Broken is a collection of mental health poetry.

These poems on mental health range from spiritual pleas to talking about the hard things.

Read more at https://adamlevonbrown.wixsite.com/ AdamLevonBrownPoetry.

---

1. https://books2read.com/u/4AGR70

2. https://books2read.com/u/4AGR70

Also by Adam Levon Brown

The Madman Speaks
The Madman Speaks Volume 1
The Madman Speaks Volume 2
The Madman Speaks Volume 3

Verses Of The Broken
Anima
Anima Yields To No One
BENT
Bent, But Not Broken - Tired, But Not Dead
Breaking Fire, Unending Quiet
Breaking Hearts Like Beer Bottles
Breaking Time Itself
Creation Lilts to Whispers of Dawn
Darkened Meadows Call My Name
Dead Hands Of Time Swing Just for Me
Emotional Explosives
Musings of An Estranged Mind
Quod Tres Veritates
Separation Of Gods
Sitting Cross-Legged Next To Misery
Standing On Everest Screaming For Dali

The Moon Is a G-Clef Caught In My Mouth
The Nightly Die - In
(Un)Broken
War Of Words

Standalone
The Journey of the Muse
Thirty-Seven Screams to Finally Let You Go
The Nameless and Forgotten

Watch for more at https://adamlevonbrown.wixsite.com/
AdamLevonBrownPoetry.